52 WEEKS OF

Faithful

PRAYER, REFLECTION,

Moments

AND INTENTIONAL
TIME WITH GOD

JESSICA A. SMITH

PRETTY PEACOCK
PUBLISHING

FAITHFUL MOMENTS
52 Weeks of Prayer, Reflection, and Intentional Time with God

The information in this book is based on the author's knowledge, experience, and opinions. The methods described in this book are not intended to be a definitive set of instructions. You may discover other methods and materials to accomplish the same end result. Your results may differ.

Paperback ISBN: 979-8-218-42465-7

Pretty Peacock Publishing
Saint Rose, LA

Printed in the United States of America
First Edition, July 2024

Cover Design by: Make Your Mark Publishing Solutions
Interior Layout: Make Your Mark Publishing Solutions

CONTENTS

SECTION 1: FOUNDATIONS OF FAITH

1. **New Beginnings:** *Focus on God's promises for a fresh start, renewal, and the power of transformation.*

2. **Love and Unity:** *Explore the biblical teachings on love, compassion, and fostering unity within the community.*

3. **Faith and Trust:** *Delve into stories of faith and trust in God's plan, even in times of uncertainty.*

SECTION 2: LIVING IN FAITH

4. **Resurrection and Redemption:** *Celebrate the resurrection of Jesus Christ and reflect on the redemption available to believers.*

5. **Nurturing and Care:** *Highlight the divine
    perspective on nurturing relationships.*

6. **Strength and Endurance:** *Encourage readers to find strength
    in God during challenges, trials, and moments of endurance.*

SECTION 3: GROWING DEEPER

7. **Freedom and Independence:** *Explore the biblical
    principles of freedom, both spiritual and societal,
    and the responsibility that comes with it.*

SECTION 4: EXPRESSIONS OF FAITH

11. **Thanksgiving and Generosity:** *Center the month around thanksgiving and the biblical call to generosity and helping others.*

12. **Advent and Hope:** *Begin the season by contemplating the significance of Advent, focusing on the themes of hope and eager anticipation.*

DEDICATION

To my beloved grandmother, Missionary Wilma Dean Lee Allen,

This book is dedicated to you. As my first Sunday School teacher you sowed the seeds of God's Word in my heart, nurturing them with the same care, love, and wisdom you bestowed upon everything you touched. Your unwavering faith, profound spiritual wisdom, and endless guidance have shaped me into who I am today.

Your teachings extended far beyond the church walls; they were woven into the fabric of our daily lives. You taught me to seek His guidance in every step and to trust in His plan with all my heart. Your life, a testament to His grace, inspired me to walk in faith, cherish my relationship with Christ, and strive to embody the love and compassion He teaches us.

This work is as much yours as mine. The journey that inspired these pages might never have begun without your guidance. Your legacy lives on through the pages of this book and in the hearts of those you have touched. May this work reflect the light you have shone in my life and the lives of many others.

With all my love and deepest gratitude,
Your Granny Girl, Jessica

INTRODUCTION

Between the quiet moments of reflection and the bustling days of our lives, we often search for guidance, comfort, and a sense of connection to something greater than ourselves. It is in these moments that we turn to our faith. *Faithful Moments: 52 Weeks of Prayer, Reflection, and Intentional Time with God* was born out of a desire to deepen that connection, to offer a pathway for others to explore their faith and to find comfort and strength in the divine presence that surrounds us all.

Each week of this devotional invites reflection, provokes thought, and encourages a more intentional relationship with God. It is my hope that, through these pages, you will find moments of peace, insights for growth, and a deeper understanding of God's ever-present love.

My relationship with God has evolved through faithful moments, becoming the cornerstone of everything I do, giving me freedom, peace, and an unwavering foundation through life's ups and downs.

As you embark on this year-long journey, approach each week with an open heart and a willing spirit. Allow the scriptures to resonate with your spirit, revealing truths and insights tailored to your life's unique path. Let the reflections, prayers, and affirmations be the starting point for your own faithful moments with God.

With heartfelt blessings,
Jessica A. Smith

"Each morning, I lay my requests before the Lord and wait expectantly, being reminded of His unfailing presence and promise. Knowing that, in all things, God works for my ultimate good, as I remain steadfast in His love and purpose." – Jessica A. Smith (Psalm 5:3 & Romans 8:28)

Foundations of Faith

Week 1

A FRESH START

Isaiah 43:19 (NIV)

*"See, I am doing a new thing! Now it springs up;
do you not perceive it? I am making a way in
the wilderness and streams in the wasteland."*

REFLECT

In the beauty of starting anew, this verse reminds us that God is the author of fresh starts. It calls us to embrace the renewal He offers, even during challenges, knowing that His plans for us are filled with hope and purpose. As we step into the unknown of a season, let's carry the assurance that God's creativity knows no bounds and His "new thing" is tailor-made for our growth.

In every uncertainty, there is an opportunity for God to carve a path, and in the dry seasons of life, He promises to bring forth streams of His grace, replenishing and sustaining us on this journey of faith.

PERSONAL REFLECTION NOTES

_____

_____

_____

_____

_____

_____

_____

_____

Isaiah 43:19 (NIV)

PRAY & AFFIRM

Prayer

Dear Heavenly Father, thank you for the promise of new beginnings. Please help us to trust in your guidance and see the opportunities you provide for growth and renewal. May we walk confidently in the path you have laid out for us. Amen.

Affirmation

I am open to the new things God is doing in my life, and I trust that He is leading me on a path of purpose and fulfillment.

INNER CONVERSATION PROMPT

In what areas of your life do you sense God is calling you to embrace a new beginning, and how can you actively partner with Him in this process?

PERSONAL FAITHFUL MOMENT

_____

_____

_____

_____

_____

_____

_____

_____

_____

_____

_____

_____

Week 2

TRUSTING GOD'S TIMING

Ecclesiastes 3:1 (NIV)

There is a time for everything, and a season for every activity under the heavens."

REFLECT

This scripture reminds us that God has a perfect timing for every aspect of our lives. As we step into a fresh chapter, let us trust that He is orchestrating the seasons of our lives, bringing about His purposes in time. Just as nature unfolds in rhythmic seasons, our lives, too, follow a divine cadence. Embracing this truth allows us to navigate transitions with grace, understanding that each season contributes to the symphony of God's overarching plan for our growth and fulfillment. So, as we stand at the threshold of this new cycle, let's anticipate the melody God is composing in the unfolding chapters of our lives, confident that His timing is always perfect.

PERSONAL REFLECTION NOTES

_____

_____

_____

_____

_____

_____

_____

PRAY & AFFIRM

Prayer

Heavenly Father, grant us the patience to trust in your divine timing. May we rest in the assurance that each season in our lives is under your sovereign control and help us to align our hearts with your perfect plan. Amen.

Affirmation

I am trusting in the perfection of God's timing, confident that His plan for my life unfolds in the right season.

INNER CONVERSATION PROMPT

In what areas of your life do you struggle with impatience, and how can you surrender those areas to God's timing this week?

PERSONAL FAITHFUL MOMENT

Week 3
ACCEPTING CHANGE

2 Corinthians 5:17 (NIV)

"Therefore, if anyone is in Christ, the new creation has come: The old has gone, the new is here!"

REFLECT

As we navigate through changes, this verse assures us that in Christ, we are continually being transformed. It encourages us to let go of the old, knowing that through Him, we are made new. In the canvas of our lives, Christ's transformative power paints vibrant strokes of renewal, turning the pages of our story into a testament of His ongoing work in us. Each step taken in His light is a testament to the truth that, in Christ, the old has indeed passed away, and the new is continuously unfolding.

PERSONAL REFLECTION NOTES

_____

_____

_____

_____

_____

_____

_____

_____

2 Corinthians 5:17 (NIV)

Prayer

Gracious Lord, thank you for the promise of transformation in Christ. Help us release the old habits and Thoughts hindering our growth and empower us to embrace the new creation you're forming within us. Amen.

Affirmation

I am a new creation in Christ and willingly let go of old patterns that no longer serve me.

INNER CONVERSATION PROMPT

What steps can you take this week to actively embrace the changes God is bringing into your life and align yourself with the new creation He desires you to be?

PERSONAL FAITHFUL MOMENT

_____

_____

_____

_____

_____

_____

_____

_____

_____

_____

_____

_____

Week 4

SEEKING GOD'S GUIDANCE

Proverbs 3:5-6 (NIV)

*Trust in the Lord with all your heart and
lean not on your own understanding;
in all your ways submit to him, and he
will make your paths straight."*

REFLECT

This powerful passage encourages us to rely on God's wisdom rather than our own. As we navigate the complexities of a fresh season, let us lean on His understanding, trusting that He will guide us in the right direction. Trusting in the Lord is not just a hopeful stance but an active surrender, a deliberate submission of our plans and paths to His divine guidance.

In this surrender, we find the assurance that, no matter how intricate the journey ahead may seem, God's wisdom is our compass, ensuring that our paths unfold with purpose and clarity. So, as we embark on this new chapter, let's carry the confidence that entrusting our hearts to Him leads to paths made straight by His unfailing wisdom.

PERSONAL REFLECTION NOTES

_____

_____

_____

_____

_____

_____

PRAY & AFFIRM

Prayer

Dear Lord, grant us the humility to submit our ways to you. May we trust in your guidance with unwavering faith, knowing that you will direct our paths according to your perfect plan. Amen.

Affirmation

I am fully surrendering my plans to God, trusting in His guidance to lead me along the right path.

INNER CONVERSATION PROMPT

In what areas of your life do you find it challenging to submit to God's guidance, and how can you actively seek His wisdom in those areas this week?

PERSONAL FAITHFUL MOMENT

Week 5

EMBRACING RENEWAL

Revelation 21:5 (NIV)

"And he who was seated on the throne said, 'Behold, I am making all things new.' Also, he said, 'Write this down, for these words are trustworthy and true.'"

REFLECT

In anticipation of a fresh start, Revelation 21:5 resonates deeply with the promise of divine renewal and transformation. This powerful scripture reveals God's ongoing work in our lives, reminding us that He is perpetually at the helm, making all things new. It's a call to open our hearts to the possibilities that lie ahead, recognizing that every new season is an opportunity for God to manifest His power and grace in our lives. This assurance invites us to step forward with confidence, knowing that the changes and new beginnings we face are underpinned by His trustworthy and true promises.

This verse not only encourages us to welcome change but also to see it as a divine intervention aimed at our growth and refinement. As we navigate the challenges and opportunities of life, the idea that God is actively working to renew and restore offers a profound sense of hope and direction. It's a reminder that our journeys are part of a larger, divine narrative of redemption, where every end leads to a new beginning filled with God's endless possibilities. Let us, therefore, embrace each new chapter with faith, holding onto the promise that in God's hands, our lives are being transformed for the better, crafting a story of beauty and purpose from every moment we entrust to Him.

PERSONAL REFLECTION NOTES

_____

_____

_____

_____

_____

_____

_____

_____

_____

_____

_____

_____

_____

_____

_____

_____

_____

PRAY & AFFIRM

Prayer

Almighty God, thank you for the promise that you are continually making all things new. As we embark on new journeys, grant us the faith to believe in the transformative power of your renewal in our lives. Amen.

Affirmation

I am confident in God's promise to renew all aspects of my life, embracing the transformative power of His renewal with open heart.

INNER CONVERSATION PROMPT

Reflecting on the promise of God making all things new, how can you invite His transformative power into areas of your life that need renewal and restoration?

PERSONAL FAITHFUL MOMENT

_____

_____

_____

_____

_____

_____

_____

_____

_____

_____

_____

_____

Week 6

THE POWER OF LOVE

Colossians 3:14 (NIV)

"And over all these virtues put on love, which binds them all together in perfect unity."

REFLECT

Let the profound truth of this scripture deeply resonate. Love is not merely a virtue among many; it is the force that binds all virtues together in perfect harmony. Throughout the week, let your actions and words be imbued with this transformative power. Picture a fabric intricately woven with threads of kindness, patience, and forgiveness, all bound together by the unifying force of love.

May this awareness inspire you to approach every interaction with a heart brimming with the kind of love that has the power to mend, strengthen, and unite.

PERSONAL REFLECTION NOTES

PRAY & AFFIRM

Prayer

Heavenly Father, teach us to clothe ourselves in love. May our hearts be filled with the kind of love that binds all virtues together, fostering unity and compassion in our relationships. Amen

Affirmation

I am committed to embracing and embodying the transformative power of love in every interaction.

INNER CONVERSATION PROMPT

How can you intentionally express love in practical ways within your relationships this week, fostering unity and compassion?

PERSONAL FAITHFUL MOMENT

_____

_____

_____

_____

_____

_____

_____

_____

_____

_____

_____

_____

_____

Week 7
BUILDING UNITY
IN DIVERSITY

Ephesians 4:3 (NIV)

"Make every effort to keep the unity of the Spirit through the bond of peace."

REFLECT

This week, take a moment to reflect on the beauty inherent in unity amidst diversity. Remember that God urges us to strive diligently to preserve this unity through a bond of peace. Embrace the differences that surround you, acknowledging that such unity is a powerful testament to the transformative influence of God's Spirit. Consider the harmony created when individuals, each with their own unique gifts, perspectives, and backgrounds, unite in a spirit of peace.

As you navigate relationships, let the bond of peace be the glue that fosters understanding, cooperation, and a shared journey of spiritual growth.

PERSONAL REFLECTION NOTES

_____

_____

_____

_____

_____

_____

_____

PRAY & AFFIRM

Prayer

Lord, help us to appreciate and celebrate the diversity within our communities. Guide us in making conscious efforts to keep the unity of the Spirit, fostering peace and understanding. Amen.

Affirmation

I am dedicated to actively maintaining unity in the Spirit, embracing and celebrating diversity in all its forms around me.

INNER CONVERSATION PROMPT

How can you actively contribute to maintaining unity in your community, workplace, or family, especially in the midst of differing perspectives?

PERSONAL FAITHFUL MOMENT

_____

_____

_____

_____

_____

_____

_____

_____

_____

_____

_____

_____

Week 8

LOVE IN ACTION

1 John 3:18 (NIV)

*"Dear children, let us not love with words
or speech but with actions and in truth."*

REFLECT

Ponder on the call to love not merely through words but through tangible actions rooted in truth. Reflect on ways you can actively demonstrate love to those around you, embodying the transformative nature of love in action. Consider the impact of small, intentional acts of kindness and the authenticity that comes from aligning actions with love. As you navigate the week, let your deeds speak volumes, creating a ripple effect of love that resonates with the truth of God's unending and transformative love for all.

PERSONAL REFLECTION NOTES

_____

_____

_____

_____

_____

_____

_____

_____

PRAY & AFFIRM

Prayer

Gracious God, teach us to love as you love—boldly and sacrificially. May our actions speak volumes about the depth of your love within us. Amen.

Affirmation

I am love in action and I will commit to expressing love not only through words but also through intentional and compassionate actions.

INNER CONVERSATION PROMPT

How can you translate your love into tangible actions this week, making a meaningful impact on the lives of those around you?

PERSONAL FAITHFUL MOMENT

Week 9

FORGIVENESS AND UNITY

Colossians 3:13 (NIV)

"Bear with each other and forgive one another if any of you has a grievance against someone. Forgive as the Lord forgave you."

REFLECT

In our personal journey toward unity, this scripture speaks directly to our hearts. Take a moment to reflect on the call to forgive as the Lord forgave you. Extend this grace not only to others but also to yourself. Consider the transformative power of forgiveness within the context of your relationships and your own inner dialogue.

Imagine the freedom that comes from releasing grievances, both towards others and oneself. Embrace the personal growth that forgiveness can cultivate in your heart. Recognize that God's forgiveness extends to all facets of your life. As you navigate your unique path, let the Spirit of forgiveness guide your actions. This fosters unity and healing in your personal connections, including the vital act of forgiving yourself.

PERSONAL REFLECTION NOTES

_____

_____

_____

_____

_____

_____

PRAY & AFFIRM

Prayer

Lord, grant us the strength to forgive as you have forgiven us. May our hearts be free from grievances, and may we contribute actively to the unity and healing of those around us. Amen.

Affirmation

"I am choosing to walk in the liberating power of forgiveness, releasing grievances and extending grace to others just as the Lord has graciously forgiven me. I embrace the transformative journey of self-forgiveness, recognizing that forgiveness brings freedom, healing, and the path to true unity."

INNER CONVERSATION PROMPT

As you reflect on forgiveness, consider: How might embracing a spirit of forgiveness, both toward others and yourself, shape your relationships, personal growth, and path to healing in the days ahead?

PERSONAL FAITHFUL MOMENT

Week 10

GROUNDED IN FAITHFUL ASSURANCE

Psalm 56:3 (NIV)

"When I am afraid, I put my faith in you."

REFLECT

As we think about the simplicity and comforting words of Psalm 56:3, let it be a reminder to anchor ourselves in God's faithful assurance. In moments of fear, let faith be your refuge. When uncertainties arise, rest confidently in the knowledge that placing your faith in God provides a steadfast foundation. Consider the peace that unfolds when fear is replaced with unwavering trust, and let this trust guide your steps through the challenges of the month, knowing that the One in whom you place your faith is steadfast and unchanging.

PERSONAL REFLECTION NOTES

_____

_____

_____

_____

_____

_____

_____

_____

_____

PRAY & AFFIRM

Prayer

Heavenly Father, in times of fear, we turn to you, placing our faith in your unwavering love. May we find solace and strength in this act of surrender, knowing that you are our refuge and source of faithful assurance. Amen.

Affirmation

"I am consciously choosing to place my faith in God, particularly in moments of fear. In Him, I find an unshaken foundation."

INNER CONVERSATION PROMPT

Reflect on the areas in your life where fear tends to surface. How can you actively put your faith in God in those moments, finding assurance in His unfailing love?

PERSONAL FAITHFUL MOMENT

_____

_____

_____

_____

_____

_____

_____

_____

_____

_____

_____

_____

_____

Week 11

GOD'S GRACE IN TRIALS

James 1:2-4 (NIV)

"Consider it pure joy, my brothers and sisters, whenever you face trials of many kinds, because you know that the testing of your faith produces perseverance. Let perseverance finish its work so that you may be mature and complete, not lacking anything."

REFLECT

Reflect on the paradoxical challenge of finding joy in trials. This scripture reminds us that trials can lead to growth, perseverance, and maturity in our faith. Embrace these challenges, recognizing that in them, God's grace is actively at work, shaping you into a more complete and resilient individual.

As you navigate trials, consider the transformative power embedded within each difficulty, molding you into a person who stands firm in faith, fully matured, and lacking nothing essential for a purposeful journey.

PERSONAL REFLECTION NOTES

_____

_____

_____

_____

_____

_____

_____

_____

James 1:2-4 (NIV)

PRAY & AFFIRM

Prayer

Lord, grant us the perspective to find joy in the midst of trials. May we recognize the growth and maturity that come through challenges, trusting in your grace to sustain us. Amen.

Affirmation

"I approach trials with joy, aware that God's grace is molding me into a mature and resilient person."

INNER CONVERSATION PROMPT

How can you shift your perspective to find joy in the trials you are currently facing while acknowledging their potential to foster growth and maturity in your faith?

PERSONAL FAITHFUL MOMENT

_____

_____

_____

_____

_____

_____

_____

_____

_____

_____

_____

_____

_____

Week 12

SURRENDERING TO GOD'S PLAN

Jeremiah 29:11 (NIV)

"For I know the plans I have for you, declares the Lord, plans for welfare and not for evil, to give you a future and a hope."

REFLECT

In the embrace of this profound promise, find deep comfort in knowing that God's plans are intricately woven for your welfare, offering a future adorned with hope. As you surrender your plans to His divine guidance, trust in the assurance that His purpose surpasses any imagination. Recognize that God's intentions for your life are driven by boundless love, seeking not harm but a flourishing destiny.

In the surrender, discover profound peace, knowing that the author of your story holds plans that far exceed your comprehension, unveiling a future illuminated with hope and filled with purpose.

PERSONAL REFLECTION NOTES

_____

_____

_____

_____

_____

_____

_____

Jeremiah 29:11 (NIV)

Prayer

Heavenly Father, help us surrender our plans to yours. May we find peace in the knowledge that your plans for us are filled with hope and promise a prosperous future. Amen.

Affirmation

"I relinquish my plans to God, trusting that His purpose for my life surpasses my own comprehension."

INNER CONVERSATION PROMPT

In what areas of your life do you find it challenging to surrender to God's plan? How can you actively release control and place trust in His purpose for your future this week?

PERSONAL FAITHFUL MOMENT

_____

_____

_____

_____

_____

_____

_____

_____

_____

_____

_____

_____

Week 13

EMBRACING DIVINE COUNSEL

Psalm 32:8 (NIV)

"I will instruct you and teach you in the way you should go; I will counsel you with my loving eye on you."

REFLECT

As we journey through this week, reflect on the profound promise that God, in His wisdom and love, personally instructs and counsels us. His guidance is not distant but intimately focused, like a caring mentor watching over us. Embrace the confidence that comes from aligning your path with His loving counsel.

In moments of decision-making, let the assurance of God's loving eye upon you bring clarity and peace. Recognize that His instruction is not a mere roadmap but a personalized guidance system tailored for your unique journey. As you go through this week, hold onto the profound truth that the Creator of the universe takes an active role in your daily life, offering wisdom, direction, and loving counsel.

PERSONAL REFLECTION NOTES

PRAY & AFFIRM

Prayer

Gracious Father, thank you for being our wise counselor. Open our hearts to receive your instruction and guidance, and may we trust in the path you lovingly pave for us.

Affirmation

"I am committed to following God's divine guidance, confident in His loving vigilance over each step I embark upon."

INNER CONVERSATION PROMPT

In what areas of your life can you actively seek and embrace God's wise counsel, trusting that His loving eye is attentive to your journey?

PERSONAL FAITHFUL MOMENT

_____

_____

_____

_____

_____

_____

_____

_____

_____

_____

_____

_____

_____

2

SECTION

Living in Faith

Week 14

RESURRECTION JOY

1 Peter 1:3 (NIV)

Praise be to the God and Father of our Lord Jesus Christ! In his great mercy, he has given us new birth into a living hope through the resurrection of Jesus Christ from the dead."

REFLECT

Embrace the unending truth of Christ's resurrection, letting it fill your heart with uncontainable joy. Take a moment to recognize the living hope bestowed upon you through God's boundless mercy. In Christ, every dawn brings the promise of new beginnings, and with this assurance, embrace the reality of a continually renewed and vibrant life.

As you journey through the week, let the transformative power of this living hope shape your perspective, infusing each moment with a sense of purpose and joy. Carry this assurance into your daily encounters, knowing that the resurrection isn't just a historical event but an ongoing source of vitality in your own story. May this living hope radiate through your actions, bringing light to the lives you touch.

PERSONAL REFLECTION NOTES

_____

_____

_____

_____

_____

_____

PRAY & AFFIRM

Prayer

Heavenly Father, we praise you for the resurrection of Jesus Christ, bringing us a new birth and a living hope. May this truth fill our hearts with joy, gratitude, and a deep sense of the life we have in Christ.

Affirmation

"I celebrate the living hope and new birth given to me through the resurrection of Jesus Christ."

INNER CONVERSATION PROMPT

How can the reality of the resurrection bring fresh joy and hope into your daily life this week?

PERSONAL FAITHFUL MOMENT

_____

_____

_____

_____

_____

_____

_____

_____

_____

_____

_____

_____

Week 15

REDEMPTION UNVEILED

Ephesians 1:7 (NIV)

"In him, we have redemption through his blood, the forgiveness of sins, in accordance with the riches of God's grace."

REFLECT

Take a moment to reflect personally on the profound redemption that Christ's sacrifice has secured. In Him, forgiveness flows abundantly, a testament to the richness of God's grace, uniquely tailored for you. Let the awareness of this redemption be more than a concept, but a deeply personal truth that shapes your gratitude and inspires a renewed commitment to live in His grace.

As you navigate this week, let the personal reality of this redemption be a guiding light in your daily choices. In moments of challenge, find strength in the assurance that you are redeemed. In times of triumph, allow your gratitude to overflow for the forgiveness you have received. May your understanding of God's grace and redemption become an intimate part of your journey, fostering a spirit of thankfulness and a deepened personal connection with the One who offers redemption so freely and intimately.

PERSONAL REFLECTION NOTES

_____

_____

_____

_____

PRAY & AFFIRM

Prayer

Lord, thank you for the redemption and forgiveness offered through the sacrifice of Jesus Christ. May we continually live in the richness of your grace, embracing the freedom found in redemption.

Affirmation

I am redeemed through the blood of Jesus Christ and live in the abundance of God's grace.

INNER CONVERSATION PROMPT

How does the reality of redemption influence your understanding of God's grace, and how can you extend that grace to others this week?

PERSONAL FAITHFUL MOMENT

_____

_____

_____

_____

_____

_____

_____

_____

_____

_____

_____

_____

Week 16

GUIDED BY THE GOOD SHEPHERD

Psalm 23:1 (NIV)

"The Lord is my shepherd, I lack nothing."

REFLECT

As you traverse this week, reflect on the comforting truth that the Lord is your Shepherd. In His tender care, you want for nothing. Embrace the peace that emanates from being led and provided for by the Shepherd who intimately understands your needs.

Let the awareness of the Lord's shepherding presence become a source of deep comfort in your daily life. In moments of uncertainty, find solace in the assurance that you are under the watchful care of the Shepherd who knows you by name. Allow this truth to bring serenity to your heart, knowing that, with the Lord as your Shepherd, you lack nothing essential for your journey. May this realization become a constant wellspring of gratitude and trust throughout your week.

PERSONAL REFLECTION NOTES

_____

_____

_____

_____

_____

_____

PRAY & AFFIRM

Prayer

Gracious Shepherd, we thank you for your guidance and provision. Help us trust that under your care, we lack nothing, finding solace in the certainty of your constant presence.

Affirmation

I find rest in the care of the Lord, my Shepherd, recognizing that in Him, every need is met.

INNER CONVERSATION PROMPT

In what areas of your life do you find it challenging to rely on the Lord as your Shepherd, and how can you actively lean on His guidance and provision this week?

PERSONAL FAITHFUL MOMENT

Week 17

RESTORING BONDS WITH REDEMPTION

Micah 7:18 (NIV)

"Who is a God like you, who pardons sin and forgives the transgression of the remnant of his inheritance? You do not stay angry forever but delight to show mercy."

REFLECT

Contemplate the extraordinary redemption and forgiveness offered by God, as illuminated in Micah. Consider how this divine example of mercy can shape your connections with others. Embrace the joy inherent in extending forgiveness, reflecting the divine delight found in showing mercy.

As you go through this week, allow the awareness of God's limitless mercy to cultivate a spirit of compassion and forgiveness in your interactions. Acknowledge the transformative impact of bestowing mercy, not only in your relationship with God but also in the way you relate to those around you. May the joy of forgiveness and mercy become a guiding force, creating a ripple effect of grace and kindness in your week.

PERSONAL REFLECTION NOTES

_____

_____

_____

_____

_____

_____

PRAY & AFFIRM

Prayer

Gracious God, who delights in showing mercy and forgiving sins, guide us to reflect this divine example of redemption in our relationships. May we extend forgiveness with joy, echoing your mercy.

Affirmation

I engage in the redemptive act of forgiveness, finding joy in extending mercy just as God delights in showing mercy to me.

INNER CONVERSATION PROMPT

How can you actively contribute to the joy of redemption within your relationships this week, embodying the mercy and forgiveness that God graciously extends to you?

PERSONAL FAITHFUL MOMENT

Week 18

ANCHORED IN RESILIENCE

Isaiah 40:31 (NIV)

"But those who hope in the Lord will renew their strength. They will soar on wings like eagles; they will run and not grow weary, they will walk and not be faint."

REFLECT

This week, find strength in the promise that those who hope in the Lord will experience renewed strength. Embrace the imagery of soaring like eagles, running without weariness, and walking without fainting.

Let this scripture inspire resilience in the hope you have in God. In the upcoming weeks, carry the assurance of renewed strength with you, drawing on the promise that hope in the Lord is a wellspring of enduring vitality. Visualize yourself soaring above challenges, running with endurance, and walking confidently in the path laid before you. May this scripture infuse your Spirit with a profound sense of resilience and a steadfast hope that propels you through every aspect of your journey.

PERSONAL REFLECTION NOTES

_____

_____

_____

_____

_____

_____

_____

PRAY & AFFIRM

Prayer

Mighty God, we place our hope in you, trusting that you will renew our strength. May we soar with resilience, run with endurance, and walk with unwavering faith in the hope that you provide.

Affirmation

I am anchored in resilience, trusting in the Lord to renew my strength and guide my steps.

INNER CONVERSATION PROMPT

How can you cultivate resilience and endurance in your faith journey, trusting that your hope in the Lord will renew your strength this week?

PERSONAL FAITHFUL MOMENT

_____

_____

_____

_____

_____

_____

_____

_____

_____

_____

_____

_____

Week 19

NURTURING BONDS WITH LOVE

1 Corinthians 16:14 (NIV)

"Do everything in love."

REFLECT

This week, reflect on the foundational importance of love in nurturing relationships. Let love guide every interaction and decision, creating a space for genuine connection and care. Embrace the transformative power of love in fostering meaningful bonds.

Consider the ripple effect of choosing love in both small and significant moments, recognizing that every act done in love contributes to a tapestry of positive impact. May this scripture serve as a daily reminder to infuse your words and actions with the essence of love, creating a legacy of warmth and compassion that extends far beyond the present moment.

PERSONAL REFLECTION NOTES

_____

_____

_____

_____

_____

_____

_____

_____

PRAY & AFFIRM

Prayer

Heavenly Father, guide us to approach every aspect of our lives with love. May our relationships be marked by the transformative power of genuine care and connection.

Affirmation

I choose to do everything in love, creating a foundation for nurturing and meaningful relationships.

INNER CONVERSATION PROMPT

How can you intentionally infuse love into your actions and interactions this week, creating a nurturing environment for your relationships?

PERSONAL FAITHFUL MOMENT

_____

_____

_____

_____

_____

_____

_____

_____

_____

_____

_____

_____

Week 20

CULTIVATING STRENGTH THROUGH LOVE

1 Peter 4:8 (NIV)

"Above all, love each other deeply, because love covers over a multitude of sins."

REFLECT

Contemplate the depth of love emphasized in 1 Peter 4:8. Consider how cultivating deep love within relationships has the power to overcome challenges and foster strength. Embrace the idea that love can be a source of resilience and unity.

In your interactions this week, challenge yourself to express love deeply, recognizing that it not only brings joy but also serves as a powerful relief in moments of conflict. As you navigate relationships, let the profound truth of love's covering grace inspire you to extend forgiveness and understanding, creating an environment where relationships can thrive despite imperfections. May this scripture be a guiding principle, encouraging you to prioritize love in all aspects of your life.

PERSONAL REFLECTION NOTES

PRAY & AFFIRM

Prayer

Lord, teach us to love deeply, recognizing that love has the power to overcome challenges and strengthen our relationships. May we cultivate a love that covers a multitude of sins.

Affirmation

I cultivate deep love within my relationships, allowing it to be a source of strength and resilience.

INNER CONVERSATION PROMPT

How can you deepen your love for others, recognizing its power to overcome challenges and strengthen your relationships?

PERSONAL FAITHFUL MOMENT

_____

_____

_____

_____

_____

_____

_____

_____

_____

_____

_____

_____

_____

_____

_____

Week 21

GUIDING WITH MATERNAL WISDOM

Proverbs 31:26 (NIV)

"She speaks with wisdom, and faithful instruction is on her tongue."

REFLECT

Reflect on the wisdom found in Proverbs 31:26, emphasizing the importance of words spoken with wisdom and faithful instruction. Consider the impact of guiding relationships through wise and uplifting communication. Embrace the role of providing guidance and care with the wisdom akin to a nurturing mother, recognizing that the words we choose can be a source of strength, comfort, and inspiration for those around us. May our speech be a Thought of the wisdom that springs from a heart of compassion and understanding.

PERSONAL REFLECTION NOTES

_____

_____

_____

_____

_____

_____

_____

_____

PRAY & AFFIRM

Prayer

Gracious Father, guide us to communicate with wisdom and offer faithful instruction in our relationships. May our words nurture and uplift, echoing the wisdom found in Proverbs 31:26.

Affirmation

I share guidance with wisdom and offer faithful instruction, nurturing relationships with the heart of a caring mother.

INNER CONVERSATION PROMPT

In what ways can you communicate with wisdom and faithful instruction, fostering nurturing relationships in your life this week?

PERSONAL FAITHFUL MOMENT

_____

_____

_____

_____

_____

_____

_____

_____

_____

_____

_____

_____

Week 22

EMPOWERING WITH RESILIENCE AND GRACE

Proverbs 31:25 (NIV)

"She is clothed with strength and dignity;
she can laugh at the days to come."

REFLECT

Marvel at the empowering combination of resilience and grace depicted in Proverbs 31:25. Reflect on how embodying these virtues contributes to the uplifting nature of relationships. Embrace being clothed with strength and dignity, fostering an atmosphere where joy and laughter prevail. Recognize that the strength and dignity we carry act as a beacon of positivity, enabling us to confront the unknown with courage and to share contagious laughter that lightens the journey for others. May our demeanor reflect a harmony of strength, dignity, and laughter, creating a tapestry of warmth and encouragement in the days to come.

PERSONAL REFLECTION NOTES

_____

_____

_____

_____

_____

_____

_____

_____

PRAY & AFFIRM

Prayer

Lord, empower us to embrace resilience and grace in our relationships, creating an environment of joy and laughter. May we be adorned with the virtues described in Proverbs 31:25.

Affirmation

I am adorned with resilience and grace, cultivating an environment of joy and laughter in my relationships.

INNER CONVERSATION PROMPT

How can you infuse resilience and grace into your interactions, fostering an atmosphere of joy and laughter within your relationships this week?

PERSONAL FAITHFUL MOMENT

_____

_____

_____

_____

_____

_____

_____

_____

_____

_____

_____

_____

Week 23

NURTURING WITH COMPASSION

Matthew 9:36 (NIV)

"When he saw the crowds, he had compassion on them because they were harassed and helpless, like sheep without a shepherd."

REFLECT

Reflect on the compassionate nature of Christ as described in Matthew 9:36. Consider how nurturing relationships with compassion can bring comfort and support. Embrace the call to have a heart that mirrors the compassion of our Shepherd, recognizing that in our own lives, we encounter crowds—people facing challenges, feeling lost, or burdened. Let us strive to be a source of solace and guidance, just as Christ was for the harassed and helpless. May our hearts overflow with the same compassion that lifts others out of despair, offering a sanctuary of understanding and care in a world that often feels shepherd-less.

PERSONAL REFLECTION NOTES

_____

_____

_____

_____

_____

_____

_____

_____

PRAY & AFFIRM

Prayer

Heavenly Father, instill in us a heart of compassion, especially in our relationships. May we nurture with the same compassion demonstrated by Christ in Matthew 9:36.

Affirmation

I nurture relationships with a compassionate heart, bringing comfort and support to those around me.

INNER CONVERSATION PROMPT

In what ways can you demonstrate compassion in your relationships, bringing comfort and support to those who may be feeling harassed or helpless?

PERSONAL FAITHFUL MOMENT

_____

_____

_____

_____

_____

_____

_____

_____

_____

_____

_____

_____

Week 24

FORTIFYING STRENGTH WITH PERSEVERANCE

Psalm 27:14 (NIV)

"Wait for the Lord; be strong and take heart and wait for the Lord."

REFLECT

This week let's contemplate the fortifying strength found in patience and perseverance. Meditate on Psalm 27:14, encouraging us to be strong and take heart while waiting for the Lord. Embrace the transformative power that endurance can bring to your strength, recognizing that waiting is not passive but an active journey of building resilience and deepening trust. In the moments of waiting, may you find the strength to endure, the courage to persist, and the heart to trust that the Lord's timing is always perfect.

PERSONAL REFLECTION NOTES

_____

_____

_____

_____

_____

_____

_____

_____

_____

PRAY & AFFIRM

Prayer

Heavenly Father, grant us the strength to persevere and take heart as we wait for your guidance. May our endurance fortify our inner strength and deepen our reliance on you.

Affirmation

I fortify my strength with patience and perseverance, taking heart in the assurance that the Lord's timing is perfect.

INNER CONVERSATION PROMPT

In what areas of your life do you need to cultivate patience and perseverance to fortify your strength and trust in the Lord's timing this week?

PERSONAL FAITHFUL MOMENT

Week 25

ENDURING CHALLENGES WITH GOD'S STRENGTH

Isaiah 41:10 (NIV)

"So do not fear, for I am with you; do not be dismayed, for I am your God. I will strengthen you and help you; I will uphold you with my righteous right hand."

REFLECT

Reflect on the assurance of God's strength in the face of challenges, as conveyed in Isaiah 41:10. Consider how enduring difficulties with God's strength can transform your perspective, turning obstacles into opportunities for growth. Embrace the promise that God will uphold you with His righteous right hand, a symbol of unwavering support and guidance. In times of fear or dismay, may you find comfort in the knowledge that God's strength is your anchor, enabling you to navigate life's challenges with resilience and unwavering faith.

PERSONAL REFLECTION NOTES

_____

_____

_____

_____

_____

_____

_____

_____

PRAY & AFFIRM

Prayer

Mighty God, help us not to fear, for you are with us. Strengthen and uphold us with your righteous right hand as we endure challenges. May your strength be our anchor.

Affirmation

I endure challenges with the strength of God, trusting in His unwavering support and guidance.

INNER CONVERSATION PROMPT

How can you actively rely on God's strength to endure challenges, trusting that He will uphold you with His righteous right hand this week?

PERSONAL FAITHFUL MOMENT

_____

_____

_____

_____

_____

_____

_____

_____

_____

_____

_____

_____

_____

Week 26

BUILDING ENDURANCE THROUGH HOPE

Romans 5:3-4 (NIV)

"Not only so, but we also glory in our sufferings, because we know that suffering produces perseverance; perseverance, character; and character, hope."

REFLECT

Contemplate the transformative process of building endurance outlined in Romans 5:3-4. Consider how challenges can lead to perseverance, shape character, and ultimately cultivate hope. Embrace the idea that endurance is a pathway to a hopeful and resilient spirit, recognizing that every trial and moment of perseverance contributes to sculpting your character. In the crucible of suffering, may you find the strength to endure, the courage to develop unwavering character, and the assurance that hope, like a beacon, shines brightly on the horizon, guiding you through every trial.

PERSONAL REFLECTION NOTES

_____

_____

_____

_____

_____

_____

_____

_____

PRAY & AFFIRM

Prayer

Lord, help us to find glory in our sufferings, knowing that they produce perseverance, character, and hope. May the endurance built through challenges lead us to a hope-filled spirit.

Affirmation

I build endurance through challenges, allowing perseverance and character to pave the way for a hopeful spirit.

INNER CONVERSATION PROMPT

How can you find purpose in challenges, allowing them to build endurance and cultivate a spirit of hope in your life this week?

PERSONAL FAITHFUL MOMENT

_____

_____

_____

_____

_____

_____

_____

_____

_____

_____

_____

_____

_____

_____

Week 27

STRENGTH IN GOD'S REFUGE

Psalm 46:1-3 (NIV)

"God is our refuge and strength, an ever-present help in trouble. Therefore, we will not fear, though the earth gives way and the mountains fall into the heart of the sea, though its waters roar and foam and the mountains quake with their surging."

REFLECT

Reflect on the strength found in God's refuge, as beautifully described in Psalm 46:1-3. Contemplate the assurance that God is an ever-present help in times of trouble, providing a steadfast refuge. Embrace the courage that comes from trusting in His strength, even in the face of life's uncertainties, knowing that His presence is a stabilizing force when the world around us seems to crumble. In the midst of life's upheavals, may you find solace in the unshakable refuge of God, drawing strength from His unwavering presence and standing firm with fearless hearts.

PERSONAL REFLECTION NOTES

_____

_____

_____

_____

_____

_____

_____

_____

_____

PRAY & AFFIRM

Prayer

Merciful God, you are our refuge and strength. In times of trouble, please help us trust your steadfast presence. May we find courage in your unwavering strength.

Affirmation

I find strength in God's refuge, trusting in His ever-present help, even in the face of uncertainties.

INNER CONVERSATION PROMPT

How can you actively seek God's refuge and trust in His strength during challenging times this week, finding courage in His unwavering presence?

PERSONAL FAITHFUL MOMENT

_____

_____

_____

_____

_____

_____

_____

_____

_____

_____

_____

_____

MID-YEAR CHECK-IN

Dear Friend in Faith,

As we reach the midpoint of our year together through "Faithful Moments: 52 Weeks of Prayer, Reflection, and Intentional Time with God," I wanted to take a moment to check in with you. How has your journey been so far? I hope that, like me, you've found this dedicated time with God to be a source of strength, comfort, and inspiration.

By now, we've navigated themes of new beginnings, love and unity, faith and trust, resurrection and redemption, nurturing and care, and the beginnings of strength and endurance. Each week has been an opportunity to deepen our understanding and connection with God, to reflect on His presence in our lives, and to embrace the lessons He is teaching us.

This midpoint is a perfect time to reflect on the changes that have occurred within you and around you. Have you noticed a shift in your perspective? A deepening of your faith? Perhaps you've encountered challenges along the way. Remember, it's through perseverance in our faith journey that we find our greatest growth.

I encourage you to look back on the moments of revelation and the challenges you've faced. Celebrate the victories, no matter how small, and reflect on the struggles, knowing that each one has the potential to draw you closer to God. Consider revisiting some of the weeks that particularly touched your heart or challenged you. You might find new insights or feel strengthened in your resolve.

As we continue our journey, remember that God's grace is sufficient for us, and His strength is made perfect in our weakness. Let us approach the second half of the year with open hearts, ready to receive whatever God has in store for us. The themes ahead promise to enrich our faith even further, guiding us through explorations of freedom and independence, wisdom and knowledge, harvest and gratitude, and so much more.

Thank you for walking this path with me. Your commitment to this journey enriches our collective experience, reminding us that we are not alone in our quest to live a life that is ever closer to God.

May the remainder of our year together be filled with meaningful moments of prayer, reflection, and intentional time with God. I look forward to continuing this journey with you, side by side, as our relationship with God continues to evolve and enrich our lives.

In Faith and Focus,
Jessica XOXO

3

SECTION

Growing Deeper

Week 28

EMBRACING FREEDOM IN CHRIST

Galatians 5:1 (NIV)

"It is for freedom that Christ has set us free. Stand firm, then, and do not let yourselves be burdened again by a yoke of slavery."

REFLECT

As we step into this new week, meditate on the liberating truth in Galatians 5:1, emphasizing that Christ has set us free. Reflect on the freedom found in His grace. Stand firm in this liberty and resist any form of bondage that seeks to entangle you. Embrace the true essence of freedom in Christ, recognizing that it is not just a release from chains but an invitation to live unencumbered by the burdens of the past. May this week be a celebration of the freedom found in Christ's love, empowering you to walk freely on the path of grace.

PERSONAL REFLECTION NOTES

PRAY & AFFIRM

Prayer

Lord, we thank you for the freedom granted through Christ. Help us stand firm and resist any yoke of slavery. May we fully embrace the liberty found in your grace.

Affirmation

I embrace the freedom that Christ has granted, standing firm against any form of bondage.

INNER CONVERSATION PROMPT

Where in your life is it crucial to uphold the liberty granted by Christ, firmly resisting any entanglement with the yoke of slavery sin puts us in?

PERSONAL FAITHFUL MOMENT

_____

_____

_____

_____

_____

_____

_____

_____

_____

_____

_____

_____

Week 29

WALKING IN THE SPIRIT'S FREEDOM

Galatians 5:16 (NIV)

"So I say, walk by the Spirit, and you will not gratify the desires of the flesh."

REFLECT

Contemplate the guidance in Galatians 5:16, encouraging us to walk in the Spirit's freedom. Reflect on how aligning with the Spirit leads to freedom from the desires of the flesh. Embrace the empowering journey of walking in the liberty granted by the Holy Spirit, recognizing that it is a transformative process of surrendering to divine guidance. Walking in the footsteps of the Spirit, discover not just freedom from the entanglements of the flesh but also a pathway to a life marked by grace, purity, and spiritual fulfillment.

PERSONAL REFLECTION NOTES

_____

_____

_____

_____

_____

_____

_____

_____

PRAY & AFFIRM

Prayer

Holy Spirit, guide us in walking by your lead, that we may experience freedom from the desires of the flesh. May our steps align with the liberty you provide.

Affirmation

I walk in the freedom of the Spirit, experiencing liberation from the desires of the flesh.

INNER CONVERSATION PROMPT

How can you actively walk in the Spirit's freedom this week, aligning your steps with His guidance and experiencing liberation from worldly desires?

PERSONAL FAITHFUL MOMENT

_____

_____

_____

_____

_____

_____

_____

_____

_____

_____

_____

_____

Week 30

CHOOSING INDEPENDENCE IN CHRIST

John 8:36 (NIV)

"So if the Son sets you free, you will be free indeed."

REFLECT

Reflect on the profound declaration in John 8:36, affirming that true freedom comes from the Son. Contemplate the idea that in Christ, you are genuinely free. Embrace the reality of living as one who is truly free in Him, understanding that this freedom extends beyond external circumstances, reaching deep into the core of your being. As the Son sets you free, let this truth resonate in every aspect of your life, bringing liberation, joy, and an unshakable sense of identity as a truly free child of God.

PERSONAL REFLECTION NOTES

_____

_____

_____

_____

_____

_____

_____

_____

PRAY & AFFIRM

Prayer

Lord, thank you for the freedom that comes through your Son. Help us to live as those who are genuinely free, embracing the independence found in Christ.

Affirmation

I choose to live in the independence that Christ has granted, knowing that, in Him, I am truly free.

INNER CONVERSATION PROMPT

How can you actively choose to live in the independence that Christ has granted you, fully embracing the freedom found in Him this week?

PERSONAL FAITHFUL MOMENT

_____

_____

_____

_____

_____

_____

_____

_____

_____

_____

_____

_____

_____

Week 31

LIBERATED TO LOVE AND SERVE

Galatians 5:13 (NIV)

"You, my brothers and sisters, were called to be free. But do not use your freedom to indulge the flesh; rather, serve one another humbly in love."

REFLECT

As we conclude this season, reflect on the purpose of your freedom, as outlined in Galatians 5:13. Recognize that you were called to be free, not for self-indulgence, but to serve one another in love humbly. Embrace the idea that true freedom is expressed through acts of love and service, understanding that the liberty you've received is an invitation to contribute to the well-being of others. As this chapter closes, let your freedom be a catalyst for selfless love, kindness, and humble service, creating ripples of positive impact in the lives of those around you.

PERSONAL REFLECTION NOTES

_____

_____

_____

_____

_____

_____

_____

_____

PRAY & AFFIRM

Prayer

Gracious God, thank you for calling us to be free. May we use our freedom to serve one another humbly in love, reflecting the true essence of liberated living.

Affirmation

I am liberated to love and serve, humbly using my freedom to care for others in love.

INNER CONVERSATION PROMPT

In what ways can you actively use your freedom to serve others humbly in love, embodying the true essence of liberated living this week?

PERSONAL FAITHFUL MOMENT

Week 32
SEEKING WISDOM FROM ABOVE

James 3:17 (NIV)

"But the wisdom that comes from heaven is first of all pure; then peace-loving, considerate, submissive, full of mercy and good fruit, impartial and sincere."

REFLECT

As we step into this new season, reflect on the qualities of heavenly wisdom as described in James 3:17. Consider the purity, peace-loving nature, and merciful characteristics of divine wisdom. Embrace the journey of seeking wisdom from above to navigate life with grace and discernment, understanding that heavenly wisdom brings clarity and a transformative impact on your interactions and relationships. In the tapestry of this chapter, may the pursuit of divine wisdom shape your decisions, attitudes, and actions, fostering an atmosphere of peace, consideration, and genuine sincerity.

PERSONAL REFLECTION NOTES

PRAY & AFFIRM

Prayer

Heavenly Father, grant us the wisdom that comes from above—pure, peace-loving, considerate, and merciful. May we seek your wisdom to navigate life with discernment and grace.

Affirmation

I seek wisdom from above, embodying its pure, peace-loving, and merciful characteristics in my daily life.

INNER CONVERSATION PROMPT

In what areas of your life can you actively seek and apply the wisdom that comes from above, fostering purity, peace, and mercy?

PERSONAL FAITHFUL MOMENT

_____

_____

_____

_____

_____

_____

_____

_____

_____

_____

_____

_____

Week 33

GROWING IN KNOWLEDGE AND UNDERSTANDING

Proverbs 1:5 (NIV)

*"Let the wise listen and add to their learning,
and let the discerning get guidance."*

REFLECT

Pause for a moment this week and savor the wisdom echoed in Proverbs 1:5. Imagine wisdom as a lifelong adventure, where the wise are not just listeners but eager learners, continuously seeking guidance. Embrace the joy of acquiring knowledge and understanding, realizing that each nugget of wisdom adds a vibrant hue to the canvas of your life. This week, let curiosity be your guide, and may the pursuit of wisdom become a personal journey that lights up your path with inspiration and growth.

PERSONAL REFLECTION NOTES

_____

_____

_____

_____

_____

_____

_____

_____

_____

PRAY & AFFIRM

Prayer

Lord, help us to be wise listeners and continuous learners. May we seek guidance in our pursuit of knowledge and understanding, growing in wisdom.

Affirmation

I actively seek to grow in knowledge and understanding, recognizing the value of ongoing learning in my pursuit of wisdom.

INNER CONVERSATION PROMPT

How can you cultivate a mindset of continuous learning and growth in your life, recognizing the importance of knowledge and understanding in pursuing wisdom?

PERSONAL FAITHFUL MOMENT

_____

_____

_____

_____

_____

_____

_____

_____

_____

_____

_____

Week 34

APPLYING KNOWLEDGE WITH DISCERNMENT

Proverbs 2:6 (NIV)

"For the Lord gives wisdom; from his mouth come knowledge and understanding."

REFLECT

As Week 34 unfolds, reflect on the profound truth echoed in Proverbs 2:6—wisdom, knowledge, and understanding emanate from the Lord. Imagine the intricacies of life as a canvas painted with divine wisdom. Embrace the responsibility of applying knowledge with discernment, recognizing its origin in God, and may your choices and actions be guided by the divine light that shapes your understanding. This week, let the wisdom that flows from the mouth of the Almighty be a beacon, illuminating your path with clarity, insight, and discernment to navigate life's complexities with grace and purpose.

PERSONAL REFLECTION NOTES

_____

_____

_____

_____

_____

_____

_____

PRAY & AFFIRM

Prayer

Gracious God, thank you for being the source of wisdom, knowledge, and understanding. Help us apply knowledge with discernment, acknowledging that true wisdom comes from you.

Affirmation

I apply knowledge with discernment, recognizing that true wisdom comes from the Lord.

INNER CONVERSATION PROMPT

How can you actively apply knowledge with discernment, acknowledging the source of true wisdom in your decisions and actions this week?

PERSONAL FAITHFUL MOMENT

_____

_____

_____

_____

_____

_____

_____

_____

_____

_____

_____

_____

Week 35

SHARING WISDOM THROUGH GRACIOUS WORDS

Proverbs 16:23 (NIV)

"The hearts of the wise make their mouths prudent, and their lips promote instruction."

REFLECT

During this week take some time to reflect on the profound connection between a wise heart and gracious words highlighted in Proverbs 16:23. Consider how wisdom intricately influences our speech, prompting prudence and instruction. Embrace the responsibility of sharing wisdom through the gracious and instructive words that naturally flow from a heart adorned with wisdom. This week, let your words be a Thought of the wisdom dwelling within you, promoting not just understanding but also contributing to a reservoir of knowledge and guidance for those around you. May your words be a source of inspiration, kindness, and wisdom, leaving a positive imprint on the hearts of those who listen.

PERSONAL REFLECTION NOTES

_____

_____

_____

_____

_____

_____

Proverbs 16:23 (NIV)

PRAY & AFFIRM

Prayer

Heavenly Father may the wisdom in our hearts be reflected in our words. Guide us to speak with prudence and promote instruction through gracious words that inspire and uplift.

Affirmation

I share wisdom through gracious and instructive words, allowing the wisdom in my heart to shape my speech.

INNER CONVERSATION PROMPT

In what ways can you intentionally share wisdom through gracious and instructive words, allowing the wisdom in your heart to shape your speech this week?

PERSONAL FAITHFUL MOMENT

Week 36

CULTIVATING GRATITUDE IN THE HARVEST

Psalm 67:6 (NIV)

"The land yields its harvest;
God, our God, blesses us."

REFLECT

Delve into the picturesque imagery of a bountiful harvest and God's blessings beautifully depicted in Psalm 67:6. Reflect on the gratitude that naturally arises from recognizing the abundance of the harvest and the divine blessings graciously bestowed upon us. Embrace this season of thanksgiving, allowing the realization of the overflowing blessings in your life to cultivate a heart brimming with gratitude. Let each day be a celebration of the abundant harvest of God's goodness, and may your Spirit be enriched with gratitude, turning every moment into a sacred offering of thanks.

PERSONAL REFLECTION NOTES

_____

_____

_____

_____

_____

_____

_____

_____

PRAY & AFFIRM

Prayer

Lord, we thank you for the bountiful harvest and the blessings you bestow. Cultivate gratitude in our hearts as we recognize the abundance of your provision.

Affirmation

I cultivate gratitude in the season of harvest, recognizing God's blessings in the abundance around me.

INNER CONVERSATION PROMPT

What aspects of your life's harvest are you particularly grateful for, and how can you express gratitude for God's blessings this week?

PERSONAL FAITHFUL MOMENT

Week 37

SOWING SEEDS OF GRATITUDE

2 Corinthians 9:10 (NIV)

*"Now he who supplies seed to the Sower
and bread for food will also supply and
increase your store of seed and will enlarge
the harvest of your righteousness."*

REFLECT

Contemplate the concept of sowing seeds, both in the field and in life, as emphasized in 2 Corinthians 9:10. Reflect on the profound idea that God not only supplies the seed but also increases the harvest, expanding the store of seeds in your life. Embrace the beautiful connection between intentionally sowing seeds of gratitude and reaping a bountiful harvest of righteousness. Just as a farmer diligently tends to the seeds in the field, may you nurture the seeds of gratitude in your heart, knowing that they have the potential to yield a rich harvest of goodness, kindness, and righteousness in your life.

PERSONAL REFLECTION NOTES

_____

_____

_____

_____

_____

_____

_____

PRAY & AFFIRM

Prayer

Gracious God, thank you for supplying the seeds in our lives. Help us sow seeds of gratitude that lead to a bountiful harvest of righteousness.

Affirmation

I sow seeds of gratitude, trusting that God will increase the harvest of righteousness in my life.

INNER CONVERSATION PROMPT

How can you actively sow seeds of gratitude in your life, trusting that God will increase the harvest of righteousness in your character and actions this week?

PERSONAL FAITHFUL MOMENT

_____

_____

_____

_____

_____

_____

_____

_____

_____

_____

_____

_____

_____

Week 38

REAPING JOY IN THE HARVEST

Psalm 126:5-6 (NIV)

"Those who sow with tears will reap with songs of joy. Those who go out weeping, carrying seed to sow, will return with songs of joy, carrying sheaves with them."

REFLECT

Reflect on the profound connection between sowing with tears and reaping with songs of joy in Psalm 126:5-6. Consider the transformative journey from sorrow to joy that is found in the harvest. Embrace the powerful idea that even during difficult times, the harvest brings forth not only sheaves but also an abundance of joy. As you navigate the fields of life, remember that tears may be the seeds of a future harvest of immense joy. Cultivate the soil of your heart with resilience and hope, knowing that the joyous songs of the harvest will eventually resonate through the valleys of sorrow.

PERSONAL REFLECTION NOTES

_____

_____

_____

_____

_____

_____

_____

Psalm 126:5-6 (NIV)

PRAY & AFFIRM

Prayer

Heavenly Father, guide us through seasons of tears, knowing that joy awaits in the harvest. May we trust in your promise of turning sorrow into songs of joy.

Affirmation

I trust that joy awaits in the harvest, even in times of tears. I embrace the transformative power of the harvest in my life.

INNER CONVERSATION PROMPT

In what areas of your life can you trust that joy awaits in the harvest, even in times of difficulty, and how can you actively embrace the transformative power of the harvest this week?

PERSONAL FAITHFUL MOMENT

_____

_____

_____

_____

_____

_____

_____

_____

_____

_____

_____

_____

_____

Week 39

ABUNDANCE IN GRATITUDE

Philippians 4:6-7 (NIV)

"Do not be anxious about anything, but in every situation, by prayer and petition, with thanksgiving, present your requests to God. And the peace of God, which transcends all understanding, will guard your hearts and your minds in Christ Jesus."

161

REFLECT

Contemplate the enriching power of gratitude highlighted in Philippians 4:6-7. Reflect on the invitation to present every situation to God with thanksgiving, experiencing the peace that surpasses understanding. Embrace the profound idea that a heart filled with gratitude not only opens a channel for prayer but also guards against anxiety, fostering a spirit of abundance. As you navigate the complexities of life, let gratitude be your guide, paving the way for a peaceful heart and a mind anchored in the richness of God's blessings.

PERSONAL REFLECTION NOTES

Philippians 4:6-7 (NIV)

PRAY & AFFIRM

Prayer

Gracious God, teach us to approach every situation with gratitude, trusting in your peace that surpasses understanding. May
our hearts overflow with thanksgiving, guarding against anxiety.

Affirmation

I cultivate abundance in gratitude, presenting every situation to
God with a thankful heart.

INNER CONVERSATION PROMPT

How can you actively cultivate an attitude of gratitude, presenting every situation to God with a thankful heart and experiencing the peace that surpasses understanding this week?

PERSONAL FAITHFUL MOMENT

_____

_____

_____

_____

_____

_____

_____

_____

_____

_____

_____

_____

_____

Week 40

HARVESTING GENEROSITY AND GRATITUDE

2 Corinthians 9:11 (NIV)

"You will be enriched in every way so that you can be generous on every occasion, and through us, your generosity will result in thanksgiving to God."

REFLECT

Reflect on the reciprocal relationship between enrichment and generosity in 2 Corinthians 9:11. Consider the profound idea that being enriched in every way enables you to express generosity on every occasion. Embrace the beautiful truth that your generosity, whether in time, resources, or compassion, creates a ripple effect of thanksgiving to God. This week, let the harvest of your enrichment be not just for personal gain but a means to cultivate a culture of generosity, sparking gratitude in the hearts of those you touch and, in turn, magnifying thanksgiving to the Almighty.

PERSONAL REFLECTION NOTES

_____

_____

_____

_____

_____

_____

_____

_____

PRAY & AFFIRM

Prayer

Lord, enrich us in every way so that we may be generous on every occasion. May our generosity result in thanksgiving to you, creating a cycle of abundance in our lives.

Affirmation

I harvest generosity and gratitude, being enriched to be generous and experiencing thanksgiving to God.

INNER CONVERSATION PROMPT

In what ways can you actively embrace generosity, being enriched to be generous on every occasion, and experiencing the resulting thanksgiving to God this week?

PERSONAL FAITHFUL MOMENT

_____

_____

_____

_____

_____

_____

_____

_____

_____

_____

_____

_____

_____

Week 41

COURAGEOUS TRUST IN THE LORD

Proverbs 3:5-6 (NIV)

"Trust in the Lord with all your heart and lean not on your own understanding; in all your ways submit to him, and he will make your paths straight."

REFLECT

Let us reflect on the courage found in wholehearted trust in the Lord, as encouraged in Proverbs 3:5-6. Consider the boldness that comes from surrendering understanding and submitting to God, acknowledging that His wisdom surpasses our own. Embrace the profound assurance that, in courageous trust, God not only guides but makes your paths straight, paving the way for a journey filled with purpose and divine alignment. In the upcoming weeks, let the courageous trust in the Lord be your anchor, steering you through the twists and turns of life with unwavering confidence in His unfailing guidance.

PERSONAL REFLECTION NOTES

_____

_____

_____

_____

_____

_____

_____

_____

Proverbs 3:5-6 (NIV)

PRAY & AFFIRM

Prayer

Heavenly Father, grant us the courage to trust you wholeheartedly. Help us surrender our understanding and boldly submit to your guidance, knowing that you make our paths straight.

Affirmation

I embrace courageous trust in the Lord, surrendering my understanding and boldly submitting to His guidance.

INNER CONVERSATION PROMPT

In what areas of your life can you actively embrace courageous trust in the Lord, surrendering your understanding and boldly submitting to His guidance this week?

PERSONAL FAITHFUL MOMENT

4

SECTION

Expressions of Faith

.

Week 42

BOLDNESS IN FAITHFUL OBEDIENCE

Joshua 1:9 (NIV)

"Have I not commanded you? Be strong and courageous. Do not be afraid; do not be discouraged, for the Lord your God will be with you wherever you go."

REFLECT

Contemplate the call to boldness and courage in Joshua 1:9. Reflect on the assurance that accompanies faithful obedience—God's presence wherever you go. Embrace the profound boldness that comes from understanding that you are not merely encouraged but commanded to be strong and courageous in your journey of faithful obedience. As you navigate the paths of obedience, let the awareness of God's abiding presence embolden your steps, fostering a spirit of resilience, fearlessness, and unwavering commitment to His commands.

PERSONAL REFLECTION NOTES

_____

_____

_____

_____

_____

_____

_____

_____

PRAY & AFFIRM

Prayer

Mighty God, strengthen our hearts to be bold and courageous in faithful obedience. May the assurance of your presence empower us to go wherever you lead.

Affirmation

I walk in boldness and courage through faithful obedience, knowing that the Lord is with me wherever I go.

INNER CONVERSATION PROMPT

How can you actively demonstrate boldness and courage through faithful obedience, trusting in the Lord's presence wherever you go, this week?

PERSONAL FAITHFUL MOMENT

Week 43

COURAGEOUS LOVE IN ACTION

1 John 4:18 (NIV)

"There is no fear in love. But perfect love drives out fear, because fear has to do with punishment. The one who fears is not made perfect in love."

REFLECT

Reflect on the dynamic power of love in 1 John 4:18. Consider how perfect love, devoid of fear, becomes a catalyst for courageous actions. Embrace the profound idea that courage finds its roots in love and that genuine love has the power to dispel fear. As you embark on this week's journey, let love be the driving force behind your actions, fostering a courageous spirit that transcends apprehension. May every step you take be guided by a love so perfect that fear finds no room to linger, creating a space for bold, compassionate, and courageous deeds.

PERSONAL REFLECTION NOTES

_____

_____

_____

_____

_____

_____

_____

_____

PRAY & AFFIRM

Prayer

Lord, fill us with perfect love that casts out fear. May we exhibit courageous love in our actions, knowing that fear has no place where love abounds.

Affirmation

I demonstrate courageous love in action, knowing that perfect love drives out fear.

INNER CONVERSATION PROMPT

In what ways can you actively demonstrate courageous love in your actions, trusting in the transformative power of perfect love this week?

PERSONAL FAITHFUL MOMENT

_____

_____

_____

_____

_____

_____

_____

_____

_____

_____

_____

_____

Week 44

BOLD WITNESS IN THE FACE OF ADVERSITY

Acts 4:29 (NIV)

"Now, Lord, consider their threats and enable your servants to speak your word with great boldness."

REFLECT

Contemplate the remarkable boldness in the face of adversity found in Acts 4:29. Reflect on the prayer for strength to speak God's word with great boldness, uttered amid challenges and threats. Embrace the courage to boldly witness for God, even when faced with daunting circumstances. As you delve into this week, may the Spirit of Acts 4:29 inspire you to stand firm in your faith, seeking divine enablement to speak the truth with unwavering boldness, regardless of the challenges that may arise. May your testimony be a testament to the transformative power of bold and courageous witness in the face of adversity.

PERSONAL REFLECTION NOTES

_____

_____

_____

_____

_____

_____

_____

_____

PRAY & AFFIRM

Prayer

Heavenly Father, empower us to speak your word with great boldness, even in the face of adversity. Consider the threats and grant us the courage to be bold witnesses for you.

Affirmation

I stand as a bold witness for God, speaking His word with great boldness, even in the face of adversity.

INNER CONVERSATION PROMPT

In what situations can you actively stand as a bold witness for God, speaking His word with great boldness, even in the face of adversity this week?

PERSONAL FAITHFUL MOMENT

Week 45

APPROACHING GOD WITH GRATEFUL HEARTS

Psalm 100:4-5 (NIV)

Enter his gates with thanksgiving and his courts with praise; give thanks to him and praise his name. For the Lord is good and his love endures forever; his faithfulness continues through all generations."

REFLECT

This Psalm gracefully encourages us to approach God with thanksgiving and praise, recognizing His enduring goodness and faithfulness. Gratitude is portrayed as the gateway to a deeper connection with God, fostering a spirit of worship that extends beyond mere acknowledgment. Embrace the profound truth that expressing thanks and praise opens the gates to His presence, creating an atmosphere where His goodness, love, and faithfulness resonate. In the upcoming weeks, let gratitude be the melody accompanying your worship, creating a harmonious symphony that echoes through the courts of the Almighty, establishing a lasting connection from generation to generation.

PERSONAL REFLECTION NOTES

_____

_____

_____

_____

_____

_____

_____

PRAY & AFFIRM

Prayer

Gracious Lord, as we enter your presence, may our hearts be filled with thanksgiving and praise. Help us to acknowledge your goodness and faithfulness continually. May our worship reflect the gratitude that overflows from our hearts.

Affirmation

I choose to enter God's presence with a heart full of gratitude, recognizing His enduring love.

INNER CONVERSATION PROMPT

How can incorporating thanksgiving into your worship deepen your connection with God and enhance your spiritual journey?

PERSONAL FAITHFUL MOMENT

_____

_____

_____

_____

_____

_____

_____

_____

_____

_____

_____

_____

Week 46

EMBRACING THE GENEROSITY CYCLE

Luke 6:38 (NIV)

"Give, and it will be given to you. A good measure, pressed down, shaken together, and running over, will be poured into your lap. For with the measure you use, it will be measured to you."

REFLECT

In the heart of Luke 6:38, we find a divine principle that transforms our acts of generosity into a cycle of blessings. It's a profound invitation to not just give but to give abundantly, knowing that our generosity triggers an overflow of blessings in return. As we explore this scripture, let's open our hearts to the transformative power of living out this generosity cycle. Embrace the idea that the measure with which we give sets the stage for the measure of blessings we receive. This week, let generosity be a guiding principle in your interactions, recognizing the abundant harvest that stems from a heart willing to give with love and openness. May this exploration of Luke 6:38 inspire a lifestyle of generosity, ushering in a continuous cycle of blessings and abundance.

PERSONAL REFLECTION NOTES

_____

_____

_____

_____

_____

_____

PRAY & AFFIRM

Prayer

Gracious God, as we delve into Luke 6:38, may the truth of this scripture become a living reality in our lives. Instill in us the joy of giving generously, understanding that with the measure we use, it will be measured back to us. May our hearts resonate with the reciprocal nature of your generosity cycle and may our acts of giving be a testament to the richness of your abundant blessings.

Affirmation

I wholeheartedly commit to living generously, trusting in the abundance that flows from a heart eager to share. I embrace my role in the generosity cycle, anticipating blessings that overflow.

INNER CONVERSATION PROMPT

How can you actively apply the teachings of Luke 6:38 to your daily life, fostering a lifestyle of generosity and experiencing the promised abundance? As you meditate on this question, envision the impact of living in the overflow of God's blessings through your generous spirit.

PERSONAL FAITHFUL MOMENT

_____

_____

_____

_____

_____

_____

_____

_____

_____

_____

_____

Week 47

PLANTING SEEDS OF HOPE IN EVERY ACT

Galatians 6:9 (NIV)

*"Let us not become weary in doing good,
for at the proper time, we will reap
a harvest if we do not give up."*

REFLECT

Begin to view our acts of generosity as seeds sown into the world, cultivating a harvest of hope. This scripture encourages perseverance in doing good, assuring that a bountiful harvest awaits those who persist. No matter how small, every act of generosity contributes to a garden of hope that will bloom in due season. Embrace the idea that, just as a farmer diligently tends to each planted seed, our continued acts of kindness and generosity nurture a future harvest of blessings. As we navigate this week, let the awareness of planting seeds of hope in every act invigorate your spirit, knowing that your efforts are integral to the growth of a flourishing garden of positivity and encouragement.

PERSONAL REFLECTION NOTES

_____

_____

_____

_____

_____

_____

_____

_____

PRAY & AFFIRM

Prayer

Gracious God, in the wisdom of Galatians 6:9, we find strength not to grow weary in doing good. May our acts of generosity be like seeds of hope, sown with faith and perseverance. Teach us to trust in the promise of a harvest, knowing that we will reap the abundant fruits of our kindness at the proper time.

Affirmation

I commit to planting seeds of hope through acts of generosity, understanding that each deed contributes to a beautiful harvest, and I will persist with firm trust in the promise of a bountiful reaping.

INNER CONVERSATION PROMPT

In what ways can you persist in doing good and sowing seeds of generosity, trusting in the harvest of hope that will come in due time? Consider the impact of your ongoing acts of kindness in contributing to a future harvest of blessings.

PERSONAL FAITHFUL MOMENT

_____

_____

_____

_____

_____

_____

_____

_____

_____

_____

_____

Week 48

GRATITUDE UNLEASHES MIRACLES: TRUSTING THE PROCESS

Hebrews 12:28-29 (NIV)

"Therefore, since we are receiving a kingdom that cannot be shaken, let us be thankful, and so worship God acceptably with reverence and awe, for our 'God is a consuming fire.'"

REFLECT

This week, the scripture calls for us to embrace gratitude as a miracle catalyst. As we receive an unshakable kingdom, gratitude becomes the key to worshiping God acceptably. This scripture encourages us to trust the process, recognizing that our gratitude is intertwined with the miraculous, transforming the very fabric of our lives. As you delve into this week, let gratitude be more than a mere expression—it is an acknowledgment of the unshakable kingdom we are receiving. Trust in the process, understanding that gratitude has the power to usher in miracles, allowing the consuming fire of God's presence to illuminate and refine every aspect of your journey. May a deep sense of gratitude mark this week, opening the door to miracles and worship that springs from a heart overflowing with reverence and awe.

PERSONAL REFLECTION NOTES

_____

_____

_____

_____

_____

PRAY & AFFIRM

Prayer

Heavenly Father, in the wisdom of Hebrews 12:28-29, we find an invitation to be thankful as we receive an unshakable kingdom. May our gratitude be a force that ushers miracles into our lives. Teach us to worship You with reverence and awe, knowing that You are a consuming fire.

Affirmation

I embrace gratitude as the key to unlocking miracles, trusting the process, and welcoming the wonders it brings into my life, infusing my worship with reverence for the unshakable kingdom I am receiving.

INNER CONVERSATION PROMPT

How can adopting an attitude of gratitude open your eyes to the miracles happening around you? Reflect on the transformative power of gratitude and its role in cultivating a deeper connection with the unshakable kingdom.

PERSONAL FAITHFUL MOMENT

_____

_____

_____

_____

_____

_____

_____

_____

_____

_____

_____

Week 49

EMBRACING THE ADVENT JOURNEY

Isaiah 9:2 (NIV)

"The people walking in darkness have seen a great light; on those living in the land of deep darkness a light has dawned."

REFLECT

As the season unfolds, Isaiah 9:2 becomes our guiding star, ushering in the Advent journey. It emphasizes the anticipation of light breaking through the darkness, inviting us to walk in hopeful expectation. Advent becomes a sacred pilgrimage where we await the dawn of a great light, illuminating even the deepest corners of darkness in our lives. This scripture encourages us to navigate the journey of Advent with hearts filled with anticipation and hope, knowing that the divine light will dispel the shadows and lead us into a season of renewed faith and joy. Embrace each step with gratitude, for in this sacred journey, the light of hope becomes a beacon guiding us toward the transformative joy of Christmas.

PERSONAL REFLECTION NOTES

PRAY & AFFIRM

Prayer

Gracious God, as we embark on the Advent journey, may the words of Isaiah 9:2 resonate in our hearts. Illuminate our path with the light of hope. May the anticipation of your coming fill us with joy, dispelling the darkness in our lives.

Affirmation

I am embracing the Advent journey this week, eagerly anticipating the light of hope amidst my darkness and joyfully awaiting Christ's imminent arrival with an open heart.

INNER CONVERSATION PROMPT

How can the anticipation of Christ's light transform the way you navigate challenges and uncertainties during this Advent season?

PERSONAL FAITHFUL MOMENT

_____

_____

_____

_____

_____

_____

_____

_____

_____

_____

_____

_____

_____

Week 50

THE COMING OF EMMANUEL

Matthew 1:23 (NIV)

"The virgin will conceive and give birth to a son, and they will call him Immanuel (which means 'God with us')."

REFLECT

In the embrace of Matthew 1:23, we discover the heart-stirring promise of Advent: the arrival of Emmanuel, God with us. This sacred verse holds the very essence of hope, a radiant beacon illuminating the fulfillment of God's promises in our lives. Advent unfolds as a divine invitation to tether our hopes to the tangible reality of God's abiding presence amidst us, a personal assurance that whispers comfort and joy into the core of our souls. As we journey through this week, let the significance of Immanuel sink deeply into your spirit, anchoring your hope in the tangible reality of God's companionship. May the promise of "God with us" infuse your days with a sense of peace and anticipation as Emmanuel's presence becomes the source of comfort and joy in every moment.

PERSONAL REFLECTION NOTES

_____

_____

_____

_____

_____

_____

_____

PRAY & AFFIRM

Prayer

Loving Father, as we reflect on the promise of Emmanuel in Matthew 1:23, may our hope be firmly anchored in your presence. Immerse us in the realization that you are with us in every season of life. May this Advent season fill us with the hope that comes from your abiding presence.

Affirmation

My hope is anchored in the promise of Emmanuel — God with us. As I journey through life, I carry the assurance that God's presence accompanies me in every circumstance.

INNER CONVERSATION PROMPT

How does the assurance of God's presence with us bring hope and comfort to your heart during this Advent season?

PERSONAL FAITHFUL MOMENT

_____

_____

_____

_____

_____

_____

_____

_____

_____

_____

_____

_____

_____

Week 51

REJOICE IN THE HOPE OF REDEMPTION

Luke 1:30-31 (NIV)

"But the angel said to her, 'Do not be afraid, Mary; you have found favor with God. You will conceive and give birth to a son, and you are to call him Jesus.'"

REFLECT

In the verses of Luke 1:30-31, we are welcomed into the divine proclamation of the extraordinary birth of Jesus. As this Advent season unfolds, we immerse ourselves in the same spirit of joyful expectation that Mary experienced, delighting in the hopeful anticipation of redemption. This scripture extends a heartfelt invitation, encouraging us to fully embrace the profound joy that emanates from eagerly anticipating the arrival of our Savior. In the echoes of the angel's reassuring words to Mary, find solace and joy in the realization that God's favor rests upon us. As we approach the culmination of Advent, let the anticipation of Jesus' birth fill your heart with a boundless and transformative hope, rejoicing in the promise of redemption that accompanies the arrival of our Savior.

PERSONAL REFLECTION NOTES

_____

_____

_____

_____

_____

_____

PRAY & AFFIRM

Prayer

Heavenly Father, as we rejoice in the announcement to Mary, may our hearts be filled with joyful expectation. In this Advent season, let the hope of redemption bring forth a profound sense of joy. May we find favor with you as we await the birth of Jesus.

Affirmation

I will embrace a spirit of joyful expectation, rejoicing in the hope of redemption. The anticipation of Jesus' birth fills my heart with childlike joy.

INNER CONVERSATION PROMPT

How can you cultivate a spirit of joyful expectation during Advent, mirroring Mary's anticipation of the miraculous birth of Jesus?

PERSONAL FAITHFUL MOMENT

_____

_____

_____

_____

_____

_____

_____

_____

_____

_____

_____

_____

_____

Week 52

EXPERIENCING HOPE IN GOD'S LOVE

John 3:16 (NIV)

"For God so loved the world that he gave his one and only Son, that whoever believes in him shall not perish but have eternal life."

REFLECT

In the timeless words of John 3:16, we encounter the very heart of Advent — a beautiful portrayal of God's boundless love revealed through the precious gift of His Son. As we kindle the flame of the love candle in this week of Advent, we submerge ourselves in the profound hope that blossoms from fully embracing the depths of God's love. Let the radiance of John 3:16 illuminate the essence of this season, inspiring a renewed experience of hope grounded in the immeasurable love of God. As we believe in the gift of His Son, let hope expand like petals, permeating every corner of our lives with the assurance of eternal life and the transformative power of divine love.

PERSONAL REFLECTION NOTES

PRAY & AFFIRM

Prayer

Gracious God, as we focus on the candle of love, may the truth of John 3:16 permeate our hearts. Let the Advent season be a time of experiencing the profound hope that comes from your sacrificial love. May we be transformed by the realization that your love offers eternal life.

Affirmation

I will experience hope in God's love as symbolized by the Advent candle of love. The depth of His love fills me with a hope that transcends all circumstances.

INNER CONVERSATION PROMPT

How can you intentionally experience and share God's love during this Advent season, fostering a sense of hope in your life and the lives of those around you?

PERSONAL FAITHFUL MOMENT

_____

_____

_____

_____

_____

_____

_____

_____

_____

_____

_____

_____

Week 53

CELEBRATING CHRIST'S PRESENCE

Revelation 21:3-4 (NIV)

"And I heard a loud voice from the throne saying, 'Look! God's dwelling place is now among the people, and he will dwell with them. They will be his people, and God himself will be with them and be their God. He will wipe every tear from their eyes. There will be no more death or mourning or crying or pain, for the old order of things has passed away.'"

REFLECT

As the year draws to a close and the Advent candles flicker, Revelation 21:3-4 unfolds a breathtaking tapestry of eternal hope. The pledge of God's dwelling amidst us unfurls like a banner, gracefully bidding farewell to pain and sorrow. In this final week, we are signaled to joyfully remember the enduring presence of Christ, becoming architects of a hope that gracefully transcends the confines of time. As we embrace the promise of Revelation 21:3-4, let the vision of an eternal future without tears, pain, or mourning infuse your heart with encouragement and hope. Celebrate the profound truth that God's abiding presence transforms the narrative of our lives, inviting us to step into a new year with the assurance that, in Christ, we are eternally anchored in hope.

PERSONAL REFLECTION NOTES

_____

_____

_____

_____

_____

_____

_____

PRAY & AFFIRM

Prayer

Heavenly Father, as we meditate on Your Word, may the reality of your eternal hope fill our hearts. We celebrate the promise of your dwelling place among us, wiping away every tear and bringing an end to pain. May we experience the fullness of hope found in Christ's enduring presence.

Affirmation

I celebrate the eternal hope found in Christ's presence. The promise of God dwelling with us fills my heart with an enduring hope that goes beyond the turning of the calendar.

INNER CONVERSATION PROMPT

As we approach the end of the year, how can the eternal hope revealed in Revelation 21:3-4 shape your perspective on the challenges and joys of the past year and inspire hope for the future?

PERSONAL FAITHFUL MOMENT

_____

_____

_____

_____

_____

_____

_____

_____

_____

_____

_____

_____

_____

Dear Cherished Reader,

As our journey through *Faithful Moments: 52 Weeks of Prayer, Reflection, and Intentional Time with God* concludes, I am filled with gratitude and hope. This path we've walked together, aiming to deepen our bond with God and His Son, Jesus Christ, marks not an end but a vibrant beginning to a lifelong journey of faith.

I hope this year has been transformative for you, nurturing a relationship with God that continues to grow and enrich your life. May the insights gained, and the peace found inspire you to keep this connection strong and ever-present.

I encourage you to share the journey and the lessons this book has offered with others. Your experiences can light the way for someone else, just as this journey has illuminated your path. Remember, the practice of drawing closer to God doesn't end here; it's a continuous journey, rich with opportunities for personal growth and spiritual deepening.

As you move forward, hold onto the certainty that God's love is constant, His guidance is unfailing, and His grace is sufficient for every moment. Continue to seek Him, cherish His presence, and let His word guide your steps.

Thank you for sharing this spiritual journey with me. May you walk forward in faith, filled with the love and peace of God, ready to spread the light you've found to those around you.

With heartfelt blessings,
Jessica A. Smith
XOXO

ACKNOLWEDGEMENTS

I extend my deepest gratitude to my Lord and Savior Jesus Christ for His unwavering guidance and boundless blessings. To my beloved husband, children, and parents, your unwavering support and encouragement have been a guiding light. Thank you for inspiring me to pursue my dreams and follow the path God has laid before me.

REFLECTIVE QUESTIONS

These discussion questions encourage you to reflect on your personal experiences and insights gained from *Faithful Moments*, fostering meaningful dialogue and ongoing spiritual growth.

1. Reflecting on your journey through *Faithful Moments*, what key insights or revelations have you gained about your relationship with God?

2. How has consistent prayer and intentional reflection impacted your daily life and spiritual growth over the course of 52 weeks?

3. Share a specific moment or experience from *Faithful Moments* that deeply resonated with you and influenced your perspective on faith or prayer.

4. In what ways has your understanding of God's presence and guidance evolved throughout the devotional? Can you pinpoint any transformative moments?

5. Discuss the role of community and accountability in sustaining your commitment to prayer and reflection. How have you shared your experiences with others, and what have you learned from their insights?

6. Explore the concept of trust in God's timing and sovereignty. How has your trust in God's plans been strengthened through the practice of intentional prayer and reflection?

7. Reflect on the affirmations and writing prompts provided in *Faithful Moments*. How have these exercises empowered you to align your thoughts and actions with God's will?

8. Consider the theme of resilience and endurance in the face of challenges. How have moments of adversity deepened your faith and reliance on God's grace?

9. As you look back on your journey through *Faithful Moments*, identify any areas of spiritual growth or transformation that you hope to carry forward into the future.

10. How do you plan to continue nurturing your relationship with God beyond the pages of this devotional? Share your strategies for maintaining a consistent practice of prayer and reflection in your daily life.

www.ingramcontent.com/pod-product-compliance
Lightning Source LLC
Chambersburg PA
CBHW030920120626
46554CB00001B/209

* 9 7 9 8 2 1 8 4 2 4 6 5 7 *